DECISIONS

Life and Death
on
Wall Street

Janet M. Tavakoli

A Kindle Single

Lyons McNamara LLC

Published by Lyons McNamara LLC, Chicago, Illinois.

Library of Congress Cataloging-in-Publication Data:

Tavakoli, Janet M.

Decisions / Janet M. Tavakoli

ISBN-10: 0985159073

ISBN-13: 978-0-9851590-7-8

Books by Janet Tavakoli

NON-FICTION

RISK

UNVEILED THREAT: A PERSONAL EXPERIENCE
OF FUNDAMENTALIST ISLAM AND THE ROOTS
OF TERRORISM

STRUCTURED FINANCE AND COLLATERALIZED
DEBT OBLIGATIONS

DEAR MR. BUFFETT

CREDIT DERIVATIVES AND SYNTHETIC
STRUCTURES

THE NEW ROBBER BARONS

FICTION - MYSTERY

ARCHANGELS: RISE OF THE JESUITS
"Conspiracies within conspiracies, a fast-paced thriller."
—*Publisher's Weekly*

Finance Classics

THE WALL STREET POINT OF VIEW
By Henry Clews
Annotations and Foreword by Janet Tavakoli

TWENTY YEARS OF INSIDE LIFE IN WALL
STREET or REVELATIONS OF THE PERSONAL
EXPERIENCE OF A SPECULATOR
By William Worthington Fowler
Annotations and Foreword by Janet Tavakoli

Acknowledgements

I would like to thank the many people who contributed their comments and encouragement, especially Father J. Allan Meyer, M.D., Rita Ilse Guhrauer, Catharine A. Henningsen, Libby Fischer Hellmann, William J. Mikus, David Pelleg, and Diane Piron-Gelman.

Contents

Preface

This short book shares my opinions and insights about the race-to-the-bottom culture of Wall Street, why malfeasance has not been prosecuted, and why change will be cosmetic and incremental, unless we alter the way money flows between Wall Street and Washington. It is not meant to be a comprehensive overview of my career or of the state of the global financial markets. Instead, selected examples illustrate the broader theme.

Assessments about the demeanor and character of individuals reflect my own opinions. I've tried to indicate where I am sharing my personal thoughts and conclusions, but in any instance without a clear indication that I am expressing a thought or opinion belonging to someone else, readers should assume I am expressing my own.

I have the good fortune to work with complicated people and live in interesting times. Almost everyone at the top levels of finance qualifies for a lifetime membership in Mensa. Yet the people I most respect are admirable for qualities other than their brains and money. They are at peace with themselves, have effective strategies to deal with stress that would drive other men mad, engage with the world around them, make interesting plans, have passionate hobbies, and look forward to the good things they will do with and for other people. They have cultivated a talent for living. This account is not about them; it is because of them.

"It is in the interest of those who control our energy to make it seem that the status quo is natural, right, and impossible to change. It is in our interest to figure out this is not always true."

—Dr. Mihaly Csikszentmilhalyi

Chapter 1

"Decisions, Decisions"

I fled the Islamic Republic of Iran with a suitcase, a thousand dollars, and no regrets. But it wasn't easy; I had to rebuild my life from scratch. Less than ten years later, I faced a decision that threatened to erase most of what I had accomplished, and I hesitated as I weighed the consequences.

In 1988, I lived and worked in Manhattan as Head of Mortgage Backed Securities Marketing for Merrill Lynch. I analyzed financial products, accompanied salespeople on customer calls, and spoke at seminars. Every morning I used the squawk box to broadcast a trade idea to the New York trading floor and U.S. branch offices: "sell this callable corporate, buy this tranche of a collateralized mortgage obligation," or vice versa. It was a great gig.

In our area of the vast trading floor, the curved continuous rows of desks with multi-line switchboards, Bloomberg terminals, computers, and squawk boxes rose in amphitheater-like tiers.

It was a late September morning. Everyone had a clear view of the stripper who removed her top to entertain the soon-to-be-married head options trader. The stripper finished her routine, and I shrugged it off and went back to work. My past objections to my boss had gone nowhere.

That afternoon, another stripper arrived to entertain another soon-to-be-married trader. She performed around 15 feet in front of me, in front of the men and women who worked for me, and in front of a visiting female customer, a bank portfolio manager. The spectacle was broadcast over the internal U.S. network. The music alerted everyone in the branch offices as to why business had stopped and distracted New York traders weren't answering their phones.

The stripper's face contorted in concentration. She was completely naked. She balanced on the arm of the trader's chair and thrust her hips towards his face—I suppose Sheryl Sandberg would tell her to just "lean in."

Men gathered around to watch and shout encouragement or make lewd remarks. George, my boss, was in the front of the group.

"She could lose a little weight," said a male voice to my right.

"No way," responded another, "her tits would be smaller."

A young woman who worked for me walked off the trading floor. She scooted past me with a pained expression and whispered, "I'll be back when it's all over."

Another woman who worked for me was a devout Roman Catholic. She stared in stunned, angry silence, and then hid her head behind the papers on her desk, literally burying herself in her work.

I picked up the phone to call George. In the past I had complained about strippers at work in a gutless tone that says *I feel I must say something about this, but if you are busy, I'll go away; if I'm creating a problem, I'll drop it.*

He always agreed that yes, it was terrible, but what could one really do? After all, this was a trading floor, and I was a big girl. Wasn't I? But he'd look into it.

I thought about what I'd say to him now. *This is the second time today. If these guys want to throw stag parties, why don't they do it on their own time?*

One of the traders picked up George's line and said George couldn't come to the phone, because he was busy. I asked if George knew I was on the line, and the trader said yes, he knew.

I laughed inwardly. I had fled my ex-husband's homeland, Iran, in June 1979 for the land of liberty. The Islamic Republic of Iran forced unwilling women to wear the chador, a black sheet that covered their bodies and hair. Now, back home in the USA, my college-educated male colleagues, "the best and brightest," paid a woman during business hours to put on a show with nothing on her body. In both cases men tried to control the where, when, and how of female sexuality. *This is still better than living in Iran*, I thought. But it was a false choice, and anyway, at the moment I didn't feel liberated; I felt trapped by unpleasant choices. I made my decision.

I pulled the pin and tossed the career grenade. Merrill Lynch's entire U.S. trading network heard my easily-recognized voice broadcast over the music: "I wish to apologize to the women who work with me and for me. This performance is not an indication of management's attitude to the firm's female employees."

Within seconds my phone panel was a sea of blinking white lights. I picked up a line and heard an angry trader yell: "Fuck you!" I picked up three more lines and heard variations on that theme. I thought I recognized a few voices, but none of the men identified themselves.

I picked up another line. It was George. He was no longer busy. He yelled, "What do you think you're doing? There are ninety percent men here, and they like it."

He was showing off for the other men. I told George I would get back to him, because I had to answer other calls.

The head of the Boston office called along with his top salesman. He offered to fly to New York and said he'd back me up if I needed it.

One of the traders stopped at my desk to say he was giving odds on whether I would be fired. Did I want a piece of the action? It was his way of telling me to keep my chin up. I smiled ruefully and shook my head. I had already placed my bet.

The head options trader arrived with eyes as big as teacups. He was scared for me, and he looked around as if he wasn't sure whether he wanted to be seen talking with me. He was getting married the following week, and although he hadn't requested it or hired her, the first stripper that day had been for him.

"Why did you do it?" he asked in an anguished voice. "What's the point? Why put yourself at risk? You're usually so sensible. You know your career here is over, don't you?"

Ed, the national sales manager, arrived from the other side of the trading floor. His face was a storm cloud. "I thought we had put a stop to this. It won't happen again. I'm going to take care of this."

Ed had independently pushed to get rid of strippers at Merrill Lynch. As national sales manager, his opinion usually carried a lot of weight, yet the evidence of his failure was right in front of him.

Unfortunately, none of those men ran the mortgage department, and sometimes being in the right is irrelevant. If you're a pedestrian crossing on a green light, you're in the right, but if a Mack truck runs the red and flattens you, you're dead right.

I picked up another phone line. It was George again. "Look, Janet," he spat. "This isn't a country club or high society. This is a trading floor. You might as well get used to it. No one cares about your opinion." He sounded very proud of himself.

"It may be my opinion, but it's also the law," I said mildly.

George fell silent. I looked at the second hand on my watch. Twenty seconds later he said he'd call me back.

Forty minutes later, George called me into his office. He sat behind his desk, rapidly twirling a pen between his fingers. "Of course, no one wants strippers on the trading floor."

I waited as he fiddled again, never lifting his gaze to look at me.

His voice grew stronger as he delivered what sounded like rehearsed lines. "What I'm *really* objecting to is that you used the squawk box. It's supposed to be used for trading and no other purpose. Mike wants to see you in his office tomorrow to discuss it."

Mike was George's boss and head of the Mortgage Backed Securities Department. He never missed a strip show if he could help it. I was being called on the carpet, and it was possible they would fire me for the mortgage department's newly minted felony: Unauthorized Use of a Squawk Box.

I was being Merrill Lynched.

The firm funded an army of lawyers and had a roomful of witnesses whose compensation depended on management's whim. Even my supporters would be compromised if they had to give testimony, and they wouldn't thank me for it. I had no intention of getting in the middle of a messy lawsuit, not over a stripper. But if I didn't keep up the pressure, they would steamroll me.

"I'm happy to talk to him about it," I said evenly. "By the way, does he want to have a word with whoever hired the stripper?"

"Of course not," George shot back. "How can anyone know who paid the girls? On the other hand, we know you were using the squawk box."

"I'm just surprised you were able to hear my voice at all over the loud bump and grind music," I pressed.

"Just don't take that attitude with Mike tomorrow," he said as he dismissed me with a wave of his hand. As I walked out of his office, George called after me, "He expects an apology."

The next morning I stood outside Mike's office and steeled myself before opening the door. I walked in and glanced at what he once told me was his favorite poster: an advertisement showing the horizontal contours of a nude, a wine bottle and a Ferrari 308GTB. The caption read: "decisions, decisions."

The iconic poster looked out of place in the office of this balding, overweight, middle-aged married man; there was a college dorm room wall somewhere just crying for it.

Mike eyed me coldly. "You know I've always supported your position one hundred percent. I wanted to stop it, but your broadcast tied my hands. It would have appeared to the guys that I was giving in to your demands. You're a big girl, you understand these things."

Why do George and Mike both keep calling me a big girl? I am not big and I am not a girl; I am an adult. I suppressed my flash of irritation and left that thought unexpressed. "I know you've always supported my point of view, and I'm sorry if anything I've done has inconvenienced you." I should have stopped there, but I soldiered on. "I don't recall broadcasting any demands, however."

"Do you realize," he said angrily, "that my boss might have heard you? Do you know what kind of a position that would have put me in?"

"Yes," I said, "I completely understand how awkward you must feel."

Mike grudgingly spoke again. "There will be no more strippers on the trading floor, and I don't ever want to hear anything more on the subject."

He didn't need to add that my career in the mortgage department was over. Years later I looked back on my decision to defy Merrill's status quo as one of many incidents in my career that informed my resolve to stand up to slick bullies spouting false narratives. It is counterintuitive, but the more tension-filled situations with uncertain outcomes one confronts, the easier it becomes to handle them. At that moment, however, I thought I had killed my career. I did not yet know that my abandonment of unwholesome appeasement was responsible for an exciting new beginning that would put me in a front row seat during the biggest financial crisis in world history.

Chapter 2

Decision to Escalate

If it hadn't been for the mortgage department's final on-the-job stag party, I never would have worked under Edson Mitchell and Bill Broeksmit, who reported to Edson. It took about ten minutes after the squawk box episode for the entire trading floor to know I was up for grabs, and after having a good laugh at my expense, Merrill's interest rate swap desk, at the time one of Wall Street's most prestigious and profitable, snapped me up.

Each department in Merrill Lynch Capital Markets was its own fiefdom with its own profit and loss statement, and departments did business with outside customers and with each other. Merrill's Japanese and European customers bought mortgage backed securities that paid fixed rate coupons, and they wanted floating rate payments, so I had done trades with the interest rate swap desk. The swaps traders were confounded by the uncertain cash flows and delay days peculiar to mortgage backed securities, so I put scenarios into spreadsheets for each trade to show the traders and customers the probable returns. The swap desk wanted to do more of that business, and my skills came in handy.

Edson Mitchell was chairman of Merrill Lynch Derivatives Products and oversaw the fixed income derivatives operation, including interest rate swaps. He was a competent, quiet man who sometimes blushed red and became tongue-tied when he talked to women. He relied heavily on Bill Broeksmit, my boss's boss, who headed the various businesses of the interest rate swap desk and related derivatives.

Bill came to Merrill Lynch from Continental Bank in Chicago. We both grew up in the Chicago area and got our MBAs from the University of Chicago a couple of years apart. We didn't know each other then, but our history gave us something in common in New York.

Bill asked me to head up the asset swap desk, and we spoke almost every day. The business had never made money in the past, but mortgage backed securities created new demand. I knew how to swap mortgage cash flows and other peculiar fixed income products, and the trades were money-makers. As word got around, everyone in Merrill's candy store knocked on our door, and we were profitable from day one.

Whenever there was a problem, it had nothing to do with the swap. It was always a credit problem, and almost all of the serious credit problems for investment grade bonds involved fraud. The rating agencies were no help; I had to look at the credits myself.

One co-op loan-backed bond was sliced into investments that got top credit ratings because of insurance from a so-called AAA bond insurer. But most of the co-op units hadn't been sold, and it looked as if the underlying commitments to buy weren't real commitments at all. The developer had stretched the truth beyond recognition. That meant the bonds would have less cash flow than the credit rating agencies assumed.

The bond insurance didn't give much comfort, either. If the securitization defaulted on payments, the insurer would only step in to make up the difference after the bankruptcy process was over. What was really astonishing was that the bond insurer didn't have much capital, yet the credit rating agencies rated it "AAA."

I discussed the phony ratings with Bill after we swapped the coupons of the co-op loan securitization. We agreed to clearly disclose the risks—including my reservations about the ratings—and let customers make up their own minds. It took a while to sell the deal, but Merrill had a lot of customers with a high appetite for risk. In the end, they got burned.

That wasn't all we discussed. I worked on a novel in my limited spare time, *Archangels: Rise of the Jesuits*—a murder mystery that I copyrighted in 1993 and kept in a box until I updated and published it in late 2012. Part of the plot involved the suspicious death of banker Roberto Calvi, the former head of Milan-based Banco Ambrosiano.

In June 1982, after $1.3 billion of depositors' money went missing, Calvi fled Rome with a suitcase full of documents amid allegations of embezzlement and mafia ties. A couple of days later, Calvi was found hanged from scaffolding under Blackfriars Bridge in London, and authorities ruled it a suicide. In 2002, twenty years after his death, modern forensic techniques determined Calvi was first strangled and then strung up under the bridge's scaffolding. Roberto Calvi was murdered.[1]

Neither Bill nor I believed Calvi committed suicide. Bill said that he'd never hang himself. It was too gruesome. He said if he ever decided to end it all, he'd "take all the pills at once," and wash them down with a great vintage; he loved expensive wine.

When the firm Drexel Burnham Lambert blew up due to aggressive and unethical practices, Bill bid on assets in Drexel's interest rate swap book at fire-sale prices. He joked that given the alleged illegal conduct, Drexel's employees should wear a "Calvi collar." The joke wasn't funny, but Bill had a way of cackling that got your attention.

Edson Mitchell left Merrill Lynch in 1995 to join Deutsche Bank in London, and Bill Broeksmit joined him a year later along with many other former Merrill employees, including Anshu Jain, who would later become co-head of Deutsche Bank, and John Winter, who left Deutsche Bank in 2001 to eventually become CEO of Corporate Banking for Barclays Bank in London. I had left Merrill in 1991, and while I occasionally spoke to or had lunch with Bill, I didn't stay in touch with the others.

Edson persuaded Deutsche Bank to invest tens of millions of dollars into personnel, offices, hardware, and software for derivatives trading. Once the bank made that decision, hiring and trading escalated. His leadership provided the momentum to make Deutsche Bank into one of the top derivatives and structured finance players in the global capital markets.

In 1997 I lived in London and worked for Bank of America. I was just about to transfer back to the United States when I got a call at home: "Janet, it's Edson..."

I said nothing as I tried to figure out how he got my home phone number at a time before the internet made it easy to find out almost anything about anybody.

"Edson Mitchell," he continued, "and I'm not selling Girl Scout cookies."

Edson's competitiveness didn't stop with the job. We had joked when he pressured the people who worked for him to buy his daughters' cookies so they could earn badges. "Yes, of course, Edson," I responded with more warmth. "What can I do for you?"

Edson had heard good things about structured trades I had done in Europe that involved sovereign bonds, tax treaties, and credit derivatives. JPMorgan was the innovator and leader in credit derivatives; Edson asked if I would join his team at Deutsche Bank to help him compete with them. Credit derivatives are leveraged bets that the credit quality of a corporate bond, sovereign debt, securitization, or other reference obligation will strengthen or weaken or that the borrower will default. For little or no money down, you could win a huge payday from a counterparty who took the other side of your bet. Back then the credit derivatives market was only around $200 billion in size and London traded only around 10% of the market. It wouldn't explode into the tens of trillions until a few years later.

Edson's call came as a complete surprise; we hadn't spoken in years. I declined. I had urgent personal reasons to return to Chicago.

At the time he called me, Edson was in the midst of a power struggle with Paul Jacobson, a former Goldman Sachs partner he had recruited the previous year to run Deutsche Bank's mortgage securities operation. I knew Jacobson very slightly when I worked at Goldman Sachs; he was brasher and more overtly aggressive than Edson. I could understand why their personalities clashed. The friction between the two men grew into a tug-of-war, and by late 1997, Edson had won the battle and Jacobson was out.[2]

But by then Jacobson had hired an ex-Goldman Sachs trader whom Edson promoted to head of global securitization. The new securitization head reportedly went mysteriously missing for days at a time, and during the Russian crisis of 1998, his profits took a huge hit. Shortly after promoting him, Edson fired him. That resulted in threats of a lawsuit, and the ex-Goldman Sachs trader won a multi-million dollar settlement from Deutsche Bank. A few years later he was arrested in an arms smuggling sting, reportedly pleaded guilty to one count of money laundering, and was sentenced to eighteen months in prison.[3]

After these events became public knowledge, Edson's call seemed less of a surprise. Perhaps he wanted people he could trust to be his eyes and ears, and my knowledge of mortgage backed securities and the global securitization market would have been as useful to him as my knowledge of the credit derivatives market.

In 1998, I wrote the first trade book to warn about the peculiar risks, *Credit Derivatives: Instruments and Applications*.[4] Deutsche Bank bought 600 copies hot off the presses and distributed them to its customers, and then the bank bought even more. I wondered if Edson was the eager buyer, but I never asked him. Our London phone call was the last time I spoke to him before he died.

Chapter 3

A Way of Life

Three days before Christmas of 2000, Edson Mitchell, head of global markets and member of the board of Deutsche Bank, packed his suitcases, walked out of the London residence he shared with his mistress, and took his final flight to the United States to spend the holiday with his wife and five children.[5]

For the final leg of his journey, Edson arranged private local transportation in his home state of Maine. On a dark cloudy snowy night, he boarded a doomed twin-engine Beechcraft King Air 200. The plane crashed just below the summit of Beaver Mountain.[6] Edson was forty-seven. Unlike his mistress, many of his financial assets were mentioned in his family's paid death notice.[7]

After Edson Mitchell's untimely death, financial reporters lauded his expansion of Deutsche Bank's global derivatives and securitization businesses. They hyped stories of his rumored £17 million ($26 million) in pay the prior year, credited him as a great motivator, and touted his love of private planes, sleek boats, and fast cars.[8] If you read the press reports, you would have thought Edson walked on water. It was only after his ex-trader's arrest for unconnected-to-Edson alleged money laundering that the fickle financial press dared use the word "notorious"[9] to describe Edson.

When I read the news reports of his death I immediately thought, *the game is afoot*. Several newspapers reported gossip about Edson's mistress and included details: they lived together in London; she was French; Edson had taken her to Deutsche Bank's large Christmas party for his employees. The first reporter would have needed two reliable sources, and the reporter would have had to ask, *how do you know*? Lots of people were blabbing.

The newspapers tried to position the mistress as a status symbol. Edson was rich and "powerful," so having someone on the side was supposed to be chic. But it was a dumb move by a member of the bank's board. Wall Street has failed to eradicate a small yet dangerous-to-libertines rogue faction: the Secret Society of People Who Deeply and Unfashionably Love Their Spouses. They felt that if Edson wanted to show off his mistress, he should have introduced her to his own spouse, not theirs. But the leaks about Edson's private life didn't seem to come from them. The blabbers seemed to be from a different faction: bonus seekers who loudly applauded Edson's "superior" values when he was alive, but now that he was dead, they wanted to exploit the temporary power vacuum. European bank boards don't care about mistresses, but they detest indiscretion. Rumor mongers were hard at work trying to gain advantage by discrediting Edson's memory; Deutsche Bank's managers were already jockeying for a better position.

When Edson died in 2000, most of the financial media thought Deutsche Bank was a powerhouse, at the apex of financial innovation. But notional amounts in credit derivatives alone were less than $1 trillion in 2000. By the 2008 financial crisis, credit derivatives had grown more than fifty-fold with London grabbing more than 50% market share, and securitizations had ballooned by around 1,600% into much riskier structures. Within a few years, Edson faded from media memory like one of the quaint old guard from the stodgy past.

Deutsche Bank was poised to become a major derivatives player. It piled risk on its balance sheet and created the illusion of solid, growing profits, just like many other large global financial institutions.

Structured financial products and derivatives were the fastest-growing products in the global financial markets in the early years of the 21st century. Departments grew exponentially and contributed one-third or more of revenues and fake profits for investment banks.

Structured finance professionals loved credit derivatives. It took zero skill to abuse the balance sheet of a strong financial institution and earn millions of dollars in bonuses. If you use credit derivatives to write protection, you take in money right away. You have revenues and you look profitable, even if you horrendously mispriced risk. Banks gave control of their highly rated balance sheets to people who piled risk onto them for absurdly low fees. It was like having your teenager sell a spin in your Ferrari for a dollar per ride. The more rides he sells, the more money he makes, until he wrecks your Ferrari.

Men in their twenties walked away with millions, set for life. Their bosses grew richer—much richer—and earned more money than they ever thought possible when they began their careers.

One of the classic indicators of fraud is fast growth where profits appear out of thin air, yet accountants pretended that this new rapidly growing revenue stream did not require a rigorous audit. Top management pretended not to know anything was amiss, even though under Sarbanes-Oxley laws, passed after the 2001 Enron bankruptcy, they were obliged to understand financial statements and risk statements before signing off on them.

*****

The banking model had huge flaws even before the derivatives explosion, and taxpayers bailed out banks before the 21st century, but derivatives amplified the risks and bailout costs soared so high that they became a huge drag on the U.S. economy.

Under the classical banking model, the golden rules were lend short, borrow long, and spread deposits among the largest possible number of depositors. Having a large number of diverse depositors makes it unlikely everyone will ask for their money back at once. Also, the Federal Deposit Insurance Corporation (FDIC), instituted in the 1930s, was supposed to stop bank runs by protecting small depositors. As for the banks, other big banks insured them.

The U.S. went off the gold standard in August 1971. With no benchmark, central banks could print money and debase currencies. That opened the door for huge bailouts after big banks screwed up in a big way. Taxpayers—not incompetent bankers—paid the price.

Before the Fed allowed banks to become too-big-to-fail, U.S. banks were vulnerable, because the U.S. imported savings to fund the budget deficit and private sector capital. Banks took in large foreign deposits, especially overnight deposits that could be yanked back.

In mid-May 1984, the Japanese found out that Bill Broeksmit's old employer, Continental Illinois Bank and Trust Company, had made unwise oil-related loans. The financial markets were in turmoil amid allegations of fraud, poor record keeping, and illegal kickbacks. The Japanese yanked back $2 billion of overnight deposits, and European deposits marched out the door right after them.

The FDIC, Treasury and the Federal Reserve Bank gave Continental Bank $5.5 billion of new capital and $8 billion in emergency loans. At the time, it was the largest bank failure in the history of the United States.[10] The judge who sentenced two bank officers to prison cited their desire to live "a life way out of proportion to one's earnings."[11]

In the 1970s and 1980s, U.S. banks took in deposits from foreign oil producers in the Middle East and lent money to Latin American countries that consumed oil. The banks charged hefty fees, of course, and paid officers handsome bonuses. Money for nothing. Everyone was on the gravy train; it was good to be a banker, and everyone wanted more. Soon they were lending other people's money like drunken sailors, irrespective of whether the Latin American borrowers could pay them back.

By the late 1980s, the loans to Latin America were seriously impaired; some countries couldn't even pay the full interest due. If the banks had honestly marked down the value of the bonds, Bank of America and Manufacturers Hanover would have wiped out their equity and then some. Irving Trust and First Chicago were also in trouble.

By now, the Federal Reserve Bank and large U.S. banks had established a pattern to control the public relations damage each time banks had a major screw-up: accountants and regulators let banks lie about the size of the problem to stall for time; the Federal Reserve blew smoke at the media; finally, the Fed would bail out the banks in a way that most taxpayers would not understand.

After the Latin American lending debacle, structured finance came to the rescue with Brady bonds, named for former U.S. Treasury Secretary Nicholas Brady. Here's how that worked. Mexico owed $20 billion it couldn't pay back. The U.S. banks that held the debt forgave half that amount. The U.S. Treasury issued a zero coupon bond that had a present value of $2 billion and a value of $10 billion at maturity, so Mexico's principal payments were subsidized, and Mexico agreed to pay the coupon interest. That's how $20 billion morphed into only $2 billion in principal plus interest. Wash, rinse, and repeat for other Latin American countries. The International Monetary Fund enabled the bailouts with minimum write-downs according to Tavakoli's Law of Sovereign Bailouts:

> Never call bad debt bad debt—at least not in public. Lend bad debtors more money, so they can pay interest on bad loans, and banks won't have to admit they have bad debt and increase reserves. When substantial "haircuts" or write-downs are involved, the banks with the most clout will determine the

size of the write-down, and they will decide when that occurs. This type of restructuring is a bailout that protects the egos, status, and bonuses of banking executives and their cronies. Done properly, you will transfer wealth from middle classes to the upper classes, preferably to bonus-seeking executives in the global banking industry.

Banks didn't have to get smarter or more competent. The Fed trained the banks to believe that uninformed taxpayers would eat the losses, and fake accounting would let bank officers keep their positions and their money.

The Savings & Loan (S&L) crisis in the 1980s was an exception to the new unwritten rule. According to investigator and regulator William K. Black, "regulators made over 30,000 criminal referrals, and this produced over 1,000 felony convictions." The worst one hundred fraud schemes involved around "300 savings and loans and 600 individuals."[12] Regulators had a ninety percent conviction rate.

At the time, I thought the S&L crisis was the final chapter in an unfortunate era in financial history, but it hardly merits a paragraph in the encyclopedia of banking malfeasance that followed. The 2008 banking crisis and the subsequent bailouts dwarfed the S&L crisis, yet no top executive at a too-big-to-fail bank has been prosecuted. Rule of law in the financial markets belongs to a bygone era when bankers were criminally indicted and sentenced to prison, instead of being invited to Congress for a love fest.

Banks had such a horrific history that you would think Congress and regulators would guide them with a firm hand. But banks bought hearts and minds in Washington. On November 12, 1999, the Clinton Administration passed the Gramm-Leach-Bliley Act that repealed the 1933 Glass-Steagall Act. Glass-Steagall had separated commercial banks that take in deposits and make loans, from investment banks that can buy and sell securities and gamble with other people's money. Glass-Steagall had also prevented insurance companies from dealing in securities.

In 2000—two years after my warnings in *Credit Derivatives* were published—President Bill Clinton signed the Commodity Futures Modernization Act that prevented over-the-counter derivatives from being regulated as futures or securities. The President's Working Group included former Treasury Secretary and former co-chair of Goldman Sachs, Robert Rubin, Treasury Secretary Larry Summers, Fed Chairman Alan Greenspan, Securities and Exchange Commission (SEC) head Arthur Levitt, and Commodity Futures Trading Commission (CFTC) Chair William J. Rainer.

Rubin, Greenspan, and Summers undermined former CFTC head Brooksley Born, claiming her advocacy of derivatives regulation would cause financial turmoil. Rubin and Greenspan told Levitt that Born, whom Levitt didn't yet know, was "irascible, difficult, stubborn and unreasonable."[13]

After the crisis, several pundits claimed that the Act meant there were no regulations for credit derivatives, but we had perfectly good laws on the books against securities fraud—whether or not credit derivatives technology was used—and against garden-variety fraud like withholding material information that due diligence could not reasonably uncover.

With Glass-Steagall gone, banks gambled with the average American's FDIC-insured deposits and used their massive balance sheets to trade derivatives and take huge risks. Banks often falsely claimed hedge funds and "off balance sheet" special-purpose entities kept risk away from banks, but the losses boomeranged back to banks' balance sheets when the market imploded.

In 2010, I gave a presentation to the International Monetary Fund explaining all of this again. An agitated senior officer gruffed: "You can't prove fraud!" I responded, "It's not that hard to prove if you investigate." In order to keep documents out of the public eye, too-big-to-fail banks were already paying huge settlements in civil cases.

The senior officer's staff rebelled, and shared their own first-hand experiences of mortgage fraud. One spoke of a housekeeper solicited by a mortgage lender who offered the woman a $500,000 loan. The staffer's husband investigated. The housekeeper couldn't have made payments on a loan half that size, and the property's appraised value had been inflated by at least double its real worth. The stories kept flowing.

Banks supplied corrupt mortgage lenders with credit lines and packaged the loans into private-label residential mortgage backed securities (RMBS). Top mortgage lenders from 2005 to 2007 included Long Beach, now part of JPMorgan Chase, with $65 billion in loan volume; Wells Fargo Financial, $52 billion; JPMorgan Chase's Chase Home Finance, with $30 billion; Citigroup's CitiFinancial, $25 billion; and Wachovia, now part of Wells Fargo, with $17 billion.

Countrywide, now a part of Bank of America, was the largest subprime lender with $97 billion in loan volume. JPMorgan Chase, Bank of America, and Citibank supplied the credit lines that made the damage possible. Ameriquest Mortgage was the second largest subprime lender ($80 billion). JPMorgan, Citibank and Bank of America supplied the money train.[14]

As securitizers, the banks were obliged to perform due diligence and to make adequate disclosures about risk. Residential mortgage backed securities (RMBS) received so-called AAA ratings for the largest chunk of each deal, because subordinated investors bore the risk of a pre-agreed amount of loan losses. But in the early 21st century, RMBSs were backed by portfolios comprising risky fraud-riddled loans. Tranches, or slices, of these RMBSs were overrated, so tranches that were supposed to be better than investment-grade often deserved junk ratings.

Wall Street disguised these RMBS losers by using them as reference collateral in new fraud-riddled securitizations called synthetic collateralized debt obligations (CDOs) that used credit derivatives to reference physical bonds. Wall Street magnified the losses by using credit derivatives to transfer the same risky losers over and over again into multiple CDOs. Synthetic CDOS are securities subject to rules against securities fraud, but after the crisis, the SEC made excuses for looking the other way for years.

I told the IMF that banks participated in widespread massive lending fraud, securitized bad loans, maliciously used derivatives to transfer bad risks multiple times, and knowingly sold misrated securities. It was fraud, a violation of securities laws.

The watchdog panel for the Troubled Asset Relief Program (TARP) had this to say about the bailouts after the September 2008 financial crisis:

> Very large financial institutions may now rationally decide to take inflated risks because they expect that, if their

> gamble fails, taxpayers will bear the loss…Ironically, these inflated risks may create even greater systemic risk and increase the likelihood of future crises and bailouts.[15]

The TARP panel restated the blindingly obvious. For decades taxpayers bailed out banks, and each bailout was bigger than the last. Billions of dollars were heart-palpitating sums in the 1970s when the government bailed out banks that got into trouble with loans to Latin America, but those billions were trivial compared to the bailouts the financial system needed in the 2008 crisis. Taxpayers were forced to provide eye-popping support amounting to trillions of dollars, and since then, taxpayers are paying more every day. The Fed prints money as if it is run by madmen, drawing on the national credit card, and no one knows how we will pay the bill.

If "rule under law" were more than just a slogan in the United States, men who occupied the senior-most positions in too-big-to-fail banks would have been disgraced, prosecuted, and jailed. But no bank executive was held accountable.

I warned about these risks well in advance. In 2003, I wrote *Collateralized Debt Obligations & Structured Finance*. It was the first—and for years the only—trade book to explain that collateralized debt obligations (CDOs) were abused, misrated, and posed substantial risks to investors and banks, especially when they were combined with credit derivatives technology. Banks and investors were taking on enormous mispriced risks.

Before the 2008 financial crisis, I spoke at seminars to the Federal Reserve Bank, the International Monetary Fund, and the CFA Institute. I spoke at industry conferences and challenged representatives of the rating agencies on public panels, and likewise challenged the false representations of so-called securitization professionals in public forums.

It was an uphill battle. To paraphrase Upton Sinclair, it is difficult to get a man to admit something, when he is paid a million dollars or more to go along with massive fraud.

It didn't surprise me that finance professionals tried to deny my assertions that these financial products were risky, opaque, and abused. The structures and the credit derivatives technology I wrote about became a playbook for malefactors to disadvantage investors who were less informed. The rating agencies participated in malfeasance by misrating securities in the way I described in my book.

Some traders recognized an opportunity for a big short, a credit derivatives trade that gained rapidly in value when CDOs inevitably plummeted in price. Michael Burry, the man Michael Lewis wrote about in his post crisis book, *The Big Short,* testified to the Financial Crisis Inquiry Commission that, among other things, he read my books before he put on his trades: "I bought Janet Tavakoli's 1998 book and that was the first book I read." The FCIC panel laughed: "That didn't sell quite as many copies as *The Big Short*."[16] Lewis's 2010 book was claptrap to catch the groundlings, and taxpayers aren't laughing. Moreover, if investors had read Lewis's finance articles in real time, they would have been misled and misinformed.

In January 2007, Michael Lewis ridiculed people who warned about risks as "ninnies" and "pointless skeptics" and incorrectly claimed there was "no evidence that financial risk is being redistributed [via derivatives] in ways we should all worry about."[17] Lewis and I were in the same training class at Salomon that he riffed in his book, *Liar's Poker*, but he wasn't looking for evidence of risk; he was merely being a smart-aleck.

Some so-called finance professionals were outraged by my early exposés of credit derivatives and CDOs. One banker in particular worked hard to discredit me, even writing anonymous negative book reviews claiming I was wrong about widespread abuse and that these securities posed little risk. I learned of his campaign when a temporary glitch revealed the names of previously anonymous Amazon reviewers. He eventually slithered onto the board of one of the two main associations for risk professionals.

Meanwhile, the market went wild. In 1997, not long before Edson Mitchell called me in London, the securitization and CDO market was only about $64 billion in size and the collateral consisted chiefly of physical cash assets. By 2002, global CDO issuance was almost $270 billion and growing like gangbusters. Credit derivatives technology enabled an explosion of synthetic securitizations that merely referenced bonds, and you could transfer the credit risk of any bond, even one you didn't own, even one that was headed for trouble. According to a Senate report on the crisis, "from 2004 to 2008, U.S. financial institutions issued nearly $2.5 trillion in RMBS and over $1.4 trillion in CDO securities, primarily backed by mortgage related products,"[18] and a large chunk of it was pure junk with "AAA" ratings.

Credit derivatives grew from less than $1 trillion when Edson Mitchell died to an estimated $62 trillion in the second half of 2007—almost ten times the size of the US corporate bond market—just before the bubble burst.

In 2010, I attended *The Wall Street Journal*'s Future of Finance Initiative in England. My analysis had been proven correct with specificity, and I was eager to hear reform proposals from bank CEOs and top professionals who attended. What often came up was anything but. In one session, bankers congratulated themselves on the survival of the banking system. They asserted that best practices allowed the chief risk officer to report to the bank's CEO, and the CEO could also be chairman of the board. In the real world, that is the definition of worst practices.

Former Treasury Secretary Paul Volcker, the man who broke inflation's back in the 1980s, explained what he thought reform should look like: a return to some form of Glass-Steagall. Mario Draghi, then governor of the Bank of Italy and Chairman of the Financial Stability Board, agreed with Volcker.

I was glad to hear it, but the feeling didn't last long. I had a drink with Paul Volcker at the post-conference cocktail party. He is 6 feet 7 inches, but he no longer seemed so tall; he was hunched over and looked tired and beaten. *Of course,* I thought, *he's making too much sense, so the powerful banking lobby will make sure he is neutralized and marginalized.* Volcker remarked that the bankers "just don't get it."

Mario Draghi is now President of the European Central Bank. In 2013, Draghi said he never thought it would be wise for central banks to sell their gold, because gold "is a reserve of safety."[19] Now Draghi prints money in the form of quantitative easing, buying banks' hard-to-fund "assets," and he no longer makes public statements in support of breaking up the large banks.

The voices of reason are being marginalized or co-opted. It's like watching a Wall Street serial horror show, *Invasion of the Ethical Banker Snatchers.*

Anyone who wanted to have an honest discussion about the causes of the financial crisis had to be shoved in a corner or silenced. Wall Street circled the wagons and made up a story for the uninformed masses. Public robbery on a massive scale requires big lies.

Citigroup, the bank that required the largest bailout, is the poster child for pulling off financial crime and getting away with it. TARP, the FDIC, and the Federal Reserve gave Citigroup $476.2 billion in cash and guarantees.[20] But the most valuable subsidy of all was the global perception that taxpayers would always be there to bail out banks.

At the beginning of June 2010, I listened to the hearings as Phil Angelides, Chairman of the Financial Crisis Inquiry Commission (FCIC) questioned former CEO Chuck Prince and "risk wizard" Robert Rubin. Rubin, former co-chair of Goldman Sachs and former Treasury Secretary under President Bill Clinton, was paid $115 million from 1999-2008 for his role as board member and strategic advisor to Citigroup, and that didn't include his stock options.[21] Both Prince and Rubin claimed they didn't know Citigroup had troubles until the fall of 2007.

Angelides asked them why they weren't worried for Citigroup in May of 2007 when Bear Stearns' hedge funds went under. He joked with the men that he remembered, because it was around the time of his birthday.

As Angelides flirted with Rubin and Prince I thought, *This is getting interesting. He's softening them up, and when they drop their guard, he's going to nail them.* But that isn't what happened.

Angelides accepted their excuses, yet Prince and Rubin knew or should have known Citigroup had grave problems in the first quarter of 2007.

Citigroup had a $200 million credit line to the Bear Stearns hedge funds. The money was supposed to be paid back in May 2007 with proceeds of an Initial Public Offering (IPO) called Everquest, a special purpose vehicle that would have been stuffed with subprime related collateralized debt obligations including some suspect tranches of deals that Citigroup underwrote. The IPO never saw the light of day, partly because of statements I had made to the press that investment in this IPO would have been unsuitable for retail investors, and it was just a way of getting around SEC rules. All of this information was in the public domain, prominently reported at the time by mainstream financial media including *Business Week* and *Bloomberg News*.[22,23]

HSBC wrote off $6 billion, including subprime losses, in December of 2006. Large mortgage lenders went bankrupt. To name just two giants, Ownit declared bankruptcy in December 2006, and New Century filed for bankruptcy April 2, 2007. In the first quarter of 2007, I publicly questioned why large U.S. banks were not taking large write-downs and wrote about it in a professional journal for risk managers.[24]

At the end of July 2010, just eight weeks after Phil Angelides' mock inquiry, the SEC alleged Citigroup deceived its stock investors:

> Between July and mid-October 2007, Citigroup represented that subprime exposure in its investment banking unit was $13 billion or less, when in fact it was more than $50 billion.[25]

Even for a too-big-to-fail bank, that was an enormous lie. The SEC charged Citigroup and two officers—no, not Robert Rubin or Chuck Prince—with repeatedly making misleading statements in earnings calls and public filings. The SEC allowed everyone to settle the charges for cash. Citigroup paid a $75 million penalty, former CFO Gary Crittenden paid $100,000, and Arthur Tildesley, Jr., the former head of investor relations paid $80,000. At the time of the SEC announcement, Tildesley was head of cross marketing for Citigroup.

I wondered how Citigroup made that decision: *We need a new head of marketing; the guy under investigation by the SEC for allegedly repeatedly making misleading statements would be perfect for the job!*

Robert S. Khuzami was the Director of the Division of Enforcement at the SEC when Citigroup paid its meager penalty. Prior to that, he was general counsel at Deutsche Bank, which was investigated by Congress for suspicious financial activities. I was astonished that Khuzami was appointed by the SEC and thought it was remarkable he didn't have to recuse himself from every securitization and earnings misstatement case, because it seemed to me he had a huge conflict of interest.

After leaving the SEC, Khuzami joined the law firm Kirkland and Ellis. According to *The New York Times*, he accepted $5 million per year to become "a paid advocate for industries he once policed."[26]

Today, Citigroup's stock trades at a price that's around 90% lower than before the crisis. That isn't obvious, because Citigroup did a reverse 1:10 stock split in 2011. Now mutual funds who cannot buy stocks trading under $5 can still buy Citigroup stock when it trades under $50, or $5 in pre-crisis pricing.

Besides, it would look really bad to taxpayers to pay hundreds of billions in subsidies to Citigroup and see the stock still trading for a few bucks a share. Multiplying the price by ten makes it look a lot less embarrassing.

When Phil Angelides brought up March 2008 and the implosion of the Bear Stearns hedge funds, I couldn't help remembering an anonymous letter written in March 2007 about a different hedge fund, and the implosion of a governor's career in March 2008.

Galleon hedge fund founder Raj Rajaratnam was tried—and later convicted—of insider trading. *The New Yorker* quoted an anonymous letter to the

S.E.C. written in March 2007 with unsavory allegations:

> Prostitution is rampant for executives
> visiting Galleon. You will find that the
> Super Bowl parties for the executives,
> paid for by Galleon Group, include
> prostitutes and other forms of illegal
> entertainment. In return, the executives
> provide Galleon the unfair edge that the
> fund leverages so well.[27]

The letter was signed: "Seeking integrity in business."

New York Governor Eliot Spitzer resigned in March 2008 after news broke that he had met a prostitute in a Washington hotel the month before. Spitzer wasn't just caught with his pants down; he was caught being a hypocrite. As New York Attorney General, he went after an international sex tour operator. His colleagues cited studies showing the average age of prostitutes entering the sex trade in the United States is fourteen. Spitzer pushed legislation to make it easier to prosecute human trafficking, calling it "modern-day slavery."[28]

The idea was to increase penalties for men who use prostitutes, squelch demand for commercial sex, and cut off the flow of money that made it possible in the first place. Yet Governor Spitzer, a former Wall Street regulator in his role as New York's Attorney General, allegedly called a vice president at North Fork Bank to ask if there were a way to anonymously wire cash.[29]

The bank officer had no way of knowing whether the hypothetical wire transfer would be to a sick grandmother, or a prostitution ring, or a drug cartel, or international arms dealers, or terrorists. The request for anonymity triggered an alarm; the bank official followed regulations and filed a suspicious activity report. It was standard procedure, even before the Patriot Act.

After Spitzer's downfall, reports revealed a pattern of behavior that went on for years costing more than $100,000 for several prostitutes, up to three in one day.[30] His former co-workers felt betrayed, and in their eyes the former governor went from hero to zero.

As the Spitzer story unfolded, I thought of his vulnerability as New York's Attorney General. In *Rough Justice*, Peter Elkind wrote that Spitzer was a client of prostitution ring Emperor's Club V.I.P. as far back as March 2006, when he was still called the Sheriff of Wall Street.[31]

In February 2008 when he was New York's Governor, he registered at Washington's Mayflower Hotel to meet the prostitute and used the name of a fund of hedge funds manager. The manager was Spitzer's friend and a contributor to Spitzer's campaign. He told the press he was "surprised and disappointed"[32] that Spitzer would use his name in this unauthorized manner, and he had no knowledge of Spitzer's extracurricular activities.

Another hedge fund manager, also a contributor to Spitzer's campaign, confirmed to the press that he had spent time at his East Hampton home with the same woman Spitzer met at the Mayflower Hotel. This hedge fund manager was a short seller who touted his due diligence in investments, yet said he was unaware that the woman he reportedly introduced to party guests in the summer of 2008 as his house sitter was a prostitute. [33] He said he never introduced her to Spitzer. The hedge fund manager was short American International Group before Spitzer began investigating the insurance giant in 2005 for accounting issues in what some thought was prosecutorial excess on Spitzer's part.[34,35,36]

Spitzer was part of a system that was supposed to be regulating both financial institutions and hedge funds, and he led a disordered life.[37] How hard would it be for someone to uncover Spitzer's secrets to manipulate him? He seemed too reckless for his former job as New York's Attorney General, much less his later job as the state's governor.

After allegations of violating his responsibilities, being deceptive, inquiring about how to disguise money transfers, acting disloyally, and becoming the epitome of hypocrisy, Spitzer still thought he could talk his way into a position of public trust. In *The Big Chill*, Jeff Goldblum's character says rationalizations are more important than sex. "We can live a day without sex, but have you ever tried to go a day without rationalizations?"

In 2013, Eliot Spitzer ran for NYC Comptroller.[38] The *New York Times* reported he was asking voters for forgiveness.[39] Spitzer obviously thought he had a shot, but he lost the primary. A majority of voters weren't interested in having him oversee the quality of financial reporting.

One of the tragedies of the 2008 financial crisis was that regulators embodied a systemic failure in their own right. Former heads of the SEC joined firms that depended on the people they had regulated for business. Other regulators either entered Wall Street's revolving door, or stayed in regulatory jobs where the key to success meant being as incompetent as possible while occasionally writing reports that few people read, much less acted upon.

Investors and taxpayers were on their own before the 2008 financial crisis, and they are still on their own, because Wall Street had its way with the USA.

In 2008, Wall Street panicked. President Bush said, "If money isn't loosened up, this sucker could go down."[40] Henry ("Hank") Paulson, former CEO of Goldman Sachs and then-United States Treasury

Secretary, went down on one knee to then-Speaker of the House Nancy Pelosi begging her to influence the Democratic Party to support the deal. Pelosi quipped: "I didn't know you were a Catholic."[41] Paulson is a Christian Scientist, but that didn't stop him from genuflecting to Congressional deal makers. Paulson helped engineer the largest no-strings-attached bailout for the global financial system in the history of planet Earth.

The only suckers that went down were U.S. taxpayers. Bailouts ultimately totaled trillions of dollars in cash, cheap funding, guarantees, asset purchases, and support.

I recognized the need for bailouts, but it was unconscionable that there were no strings attached. A lot of people saw it coming. Paulson could have done his job much earlier, but if he had, he would have had to expose a lot of his cronies for the malefactors they were. In fact, he would have had to answer questions about his own role as former CEO of Goldman Sachs.

One of the most unattractive lies of the 2008 financial crisis was that investment bank Goldman Sachs would not have failed and did not need a bailout. The report by the Special Inspector General for the Troubled Asset Relief Program (SIGTARP) debunked Goldman Sachs's story, as did I.[42,43]

The taxpayer bailout of insurance giant American International Group (AIG)[44], one of Goldman Sachs' largest debtors[45], might not even have been necessary, and this bailout—and in particular, the way it was done—was an outrageous abuse of public trust. In November 2014, Richard Teitelbaum reported that Hank Paulson dismissed a potential investment in AIG from China Investment Corporation (CIC). AIG owed Goldman Sachs and its business partners billions of dollars on credit derivatives with suspect CDOs as underlying assets. At the time, the Fed kept the details secret, but taxpayers were footing the bill and had a right to know.[46] There would have been a public outcry if it was known that at the time of the November 2008 buyout, some of the collateralized debt obligations (CDOs) had implied prices of around 60 cents on the dollar, and others had implied prices of around 20 cents on the dollar.

Dismissing CIC cleared the path for Paulson to arrange a bailout of AIG in a way that benefitted Goldman Sachs at the expense of the U.S. taxpayer, and it enabled the cover-up. Other bond insurers negotiated deep discounts with trading partners, but Goldman Sachs and its cronies were paid a scandalous windfall with taxpayer funds: the full price for suspect assets referenced by the credit derivatives, and Goldman Sachs had manufactured many of the flawed assets in its own financial meth lab. During the bailout decisions, Goldman Sachs's officers were inside the tent supposedly advising how to save the system when in fact they were advising how to save themselves. It was a self-serving conflict of interest more egregious than the various bank rescues.[47]

In 2008, Goldman Sachs was made a bank holding company, so it could borrow money at near-zero interest rates from the Federal Reserve Bank. Not only did we bail out people who should be thoroughly investigated, we rewarded failed financial institutions with near zero-cost loans. Instead of gratitude, taxpayers endured further insults as so-called executives publicly congratulated themselves as "the best and the brightest people" who deserved to be paid top dollar.[48] Yet their firms would have been history without taxpayer bailouts.

Meanwhile, individual investors and pension funds get negative inflation-adjusted rates on "risk free" Treasury bonds. Goldman Sachs aggressively repaid TARP to minimize their costs—and in particular, to get out from under the caps on employee pay imposed by TARP—in large part because of a corrupt bailout and cheap taxpayer funding courtesy of the U.S. Treasury and the Federal Reserve Bank.

To keep up the myth that Wall Street executives were the best and the brightest and not just sly operators with their hands in taxpayers' pockets, both the New York Fed and the SEC kept damaging information out of the public eye. Wall Street firms tried to fool the public about the extent of their distress.

On a September 16, 2008 conference call, Goldman Sachs CFO David Viniar said, "Whatever the outcome at AIG, I would expect the direct impact of our credit exposure [to both AIG and Lehman Brothers] to be immaterial to our results." In October 2009, I wrote that this was, in my opinion, a lie of omission.[49] Shortly thereafter, a Goldman Sachs spokesman called me with denials and obfuscations. Among other things, he claimed Goldman Sachs only acted as an "intermediary." Inadvertently or otherwise, he lied.

I wondered how often Goldman Sachs bullied and lied to the mainstream press. Most reporters brought a pen to a gunfight. Unfortunately for the Goldman Sachs spokesman, I had a list of the collateralized debt obligations against which AIG wrote protection in the form of credit derivatives. Goldman Sachs had been underwriter or co-underwriter of the largest chunk of them. That was a huge leap from just being an intermediary. As the underwriter, Goldman Sachs was obliged to perform due diligence and to disclose risks.

After the Goldman Sachs spokesman's call, I decided to make even more information public. It was the opposite of what he wanted. I broke the news that Goldman Sachs had a key—previously undisclosed—role in AIG's distress.[50,51,52]

Before he was Secretary of the Treasury, Hank Paulson was CEO of Goldman Sachs from 1999-2006, and it was under his leadership that Goldman Sachs created CDOs and entered into trades with AIG.[53,54,55] As the CDOs imploded,

Goldman Sachs's credit derivatives skyrocketed in value, and Goldman Sachs called AIG for collateral. By September 2008, Goldman Sachs had demanded $7.5 billion, and it wanted more, but AIG couldn't pay; the cash demands were the key reason AIG was going under.

Goldman Sachs claimed it was hedged through credit derivatives it bought from other banks in case AIG failed. But the fallacy with that argument was that if taxpayers hadn't bailed everyone out, Goldman's trading partners would not have been able to pay for the protection that Goldman Sachs bought on AIG. Moreover, the "protection" seemed several billion dollars short of what was needed even if the banks had been good for it, and they were not.

Goldman Sachs made a huge mistake when Hank Paulson was CEO, and as Treasury Secretary, Paulson finagled a windfall for his old firm, with no accountability whatsoever for himself or for Goldman Sachs.

The Financial Crisis Inquiry Commission's first report didn't mention Goldman Sachs's key role. I publicly said I found the FCIC's omission suspicious.[56] The FCIC's next report came out a week after I broke the news. The new report included part of Goldman Sachs's role.

In the wake of these disclosures, Senator Carl Levin led another probe and revealed that Goldman Sachs magnified losses for investors. In one example, Goldman Sachs used a $38 million subprime mortgage bond as the reference asset for credit derivatives to transfer the risk of this deteriorating bond into more than thirty debt pools of synthetic collateralized debt obligations. By this means, Goldman Sachs ultimately caused investors to lose about $280 million.[57] Goldman Sachs did this over and over with other deteriorating bonds and multiple synthetic CDOs.[58] Goldman Sachs created RMBS and CDOs it knew or should have known were overrated and overpriced when it sold them. Yet where were the massive SEC investigations?

According to the Senate report, Goldman Sachs had a conflict of interest with its own clients and used credit derivatives to make short bets that made money, while the CDOs investors purchased lost money.[59]

In 2010, Goldman Sachs was sued by the SEC for fraud and settled the matter for $550 million.[60] But the case only involved one of many suspect CDOs, and there were no criminal indictments for senior managers. A lowly salesman was the scapegoat and is still fighting the charges.

In the fall of 2009, one year after the financial crisis, Goldman Sachs put aside $20 billion for bonuses. Those bonuses would not have been possible if Hank Paulson hadn't helped shovel taxpayers' cash into Goldman Sachs (and its cronies) so it could pay back its TARP debt. Goldman Sachs courted the media to head off a public relations disaster. But it backfired in the United Kingdom. John Arlidge of the *Times of London* interviewed an exultant Goldman Sachs executive who crowed, "We've got a bigger and richer pot to piss in."

Arlidge asked Lloyd Blankfein, CEO of Goldman Sachs, whether it would continue to rake in cash getting richer than God. Blankfein grinned and replied that he was "doing God's work." In 2014, Blankfein was paid $21 million in cash and stock by his taxpayer-subsidized firm.[61]

At first, Congress put on a show that it would limit bankers' pay. After all, the financial system would have imploded without trillions in taxpayer support. On March 19, 2009, the day the House passed a bill to slap a 90% tax on bankers' bonuses, I met with Jamie Dimon, Chairman and CEO of JPMorgan Chase. The banks were still shaky. It was little more than one year after the financial crisis, and the stock market was near its lowest post-crisis level.

In August of 2007, thirteen months before the financial crisis, I had met with Dimon about the huge risks at AIG. AIG took zero accounting losses on its credit derivatives—including the Goldman Sachs trades. The *Wall Street Journal* quoted me at the time: "There's no way these aren't showing a loss."[62] AIG's spokesman called me to make excuses. The hapless man did not take me up on my offer to explain my analysis to AIG's CFO. AIG had material accounting losses that would soon be material actual losses, and AIG should have reported it. Six months later, AIG's auditor stated it found "material weakness with respect to its accounting."[63] A year later, taxpayers bailed out AIG with cash and credit support amounting to $182.5 billion.[64] Dimon said he wished he had listened to me about AIG. Now I was back to discuss a new pressing problem with Dimon, but he derailed the conversation.

Dimon was distraught that the House bill for the 90% bonus tax was on its way to the Senate. His power was intimately tied to his ability to award or deny huge sums of money to his vassals. He was also worried about JPMorgan's survival. He said more than once that if people had to double up in offices, even if he had to share the CEO's office with other bankers, he would do it.

Dimon didn't ask why I had urgently called this meeting. *Even though we had poured $476 billion in support and cash into Citibank, it was close to collapse.* The Federal Deposit Insurance Corporation never put Citibank on its problem assets list, because the Fed pressured the FDIC not to downgrade the bank and kept the whole thing secret. I later told *Newsweek*, "Citi was in much more serious trouble than people outside both the bank and the New York Fed knew."[65] But Dimon was in no state of mind to hear the reason I had asked to meet with him.

Dimon repeated talking points. He sounded obsessed and spoke as if he were reading a script: "You don't remember the recession in the 1970's, Janet, but I do. I know how to manage the bank through a recession."

I reminded him that I did indeed remember that recession and that I'm three years older than he is. Around ten minutes later he repeated himself: "You don't remember the recession in the 1970's, Janet, but I do. I know how to manage the bank through a recession."

Again, I reminded him that I remembered it well.

A few minutes later he repeated his line about the recession of the 1970s again. He seemed distracted and wasn't taking in any information. His demeanor concerned me, and I thought, *Is this what a nervous breakdown looks like? If he keeps this up, he'll blow his brains out.*

I stood up, and as he walked me to the elevator, he said that he thought he'd go home and have more than one drink that evening.

I appraised his demeanor again and thought alcohol was the last thing he needed. "If I were you, I wouldn't be drinking at all; I'd spend more time in the gym."

Dimon wasn't the only one crumbling under pressure. In September 2008, David M. Moffett resigned from the board of MBIA, the municipal bond insurer that imploded due to its exposure via credit derivatives to phony "highly rated" tranches of collateralized debt obligations. In March 2009, the same month that I met with Dimon, Moffett resigned his position as CEO of bailed-out mortgage giant Freddie Mac.

Freddie Mac's officers insisted the costs of the Obama administration-sponsored housing recovery plan be disclosed to shareholders. The Federal Housing Finance Agency (FHFA) pressured the company not to disclose the information—at least not in the way Freddie Mac's officers wanted it disclosed—in Freddie Mac's financial reports.[66]

In April 2009, the month after I met with Dimon, David B. Kellermann, Freddie Mac's forty-one year old CFO, walked down to his basement and hung himself. A Freddie Mac executive told the *New York Times*, "the pressure right now is relentless."[67]

Bailed-out banks desperately and vigorously lobbied Congress, and it paid off. In April 2009, the accounting rules were changed to make it easier for banks to hide losses.[68] The 90% bonus tax bill disappeared as money flowed from Wall Street to Congress.

Bankers spun a narrative that enormous unwarranted compensation for Wall Street employees was needed to keep "the best and the brightest." Institutions that would have vanished without taxpayer support paid tens of billions of taxpayer-subsidized bonuses. Malefactors who should have been indicted were among them.

Once again, banks didn't need to become smarter, more careful, or better managed. They didn't even need to stop some of their ongoing criminal behavior. Regulation and civil prosecutions were all for show, and taxpayers funded the fines that regulators selectively levied.

Jamie Dimon was such a shaken man in March 2009 that you'd think he would have invested heavily in risk management and worked like a demon to reform the bank. Instead, since 2009, JPMorgan Chase has been involved in a string of malfeasance and trading debacles, including, but not limited to, hundreds of millions in losses due to a wildly oversized short position in coal during wartime,[69,70] and manipulation of the electric markets resulting in a settlement of $410 million.[71] The so-called London Whale debacle resulted in more than $6 billion in losses in 2012 due to oversized positions in credit derivatives in the London-based Chief Investment Office (CIO) unit that reported to Dimon. Years of the unit's profits were wiped out. The SEC fined JPMorgan Chase $920 million, and JPMorgan Chase made an admission of wrongdoing.[72] There is still an ongoing investigation, and Dimon may not be off the hook.

During an April 13, 2012 earnings call, Chairman and CEO Jamie Dimon discredited and dismissed media reports about JPMorgan's oversized credit derivatives risk and mounting losses, calling it a "tempest in a teapot." But according to a Senate report, Dimon knew otherwise:

> While he later apologized for that comment, his judgment likely was of importance to investors in the immediate aftermath of those media reports. The evidence also indicates that, when he made that statement, Mr. Dimon was already in possession of information about the [Synthetic Credit Portfolio's (SCP)] complex and sizeable portfolio, its sustained losses for three straight months, the exponential increase in those losses during March, and the difficulty of exiting the SCP's positions.[73]

Will Jamie Dimon be indicted for making misleading statements to investors? He did not seem worried about it when he addressed the annual investors' meeting in February 2013. After bank analyst Mike Mayo asked Dimon if capital ratios matter to depositors, Dimon dodged the question, saying, "So you would go to UBS [a bank with a higher capital ratio] and not JPMorgan?"

Mayo protested that he didn't say that, only that UBS was making the argument that capital ratios may matter to depositors.

Dimon dodged again: "That's why I'm richer than you."[74]

The man who seemed to be a craven nervous wreck in March 2009 now seemed to use aggressive arrogance to intimidate the weak-kneed. The media widely reported the sound bite, but few noted that incessant self-regard is an inappropriate response to legitimate public business questions, especially after JPMorgan's post-crisis string of spectacular blunders that call Dimon's competence into question.

Moreover, Mayo didn't disclose his net worth, and the word *rich* encompasses more than money. There are qualities to richness we all have to develop on our own. Money cannot buy a man a pleasant sense of humor, money will not make a man behave decently, and money cannot teach a man how to treat others with dignity.

Chapter 4

"Irreversible Decision"

U.S. banks weren't the only contributors to the financial crisis. French, Swiss, British banks and more were also mired in the mess. The Senate investigation into the financial crisis revealed Deutsche Bank sold CDOs without full disclosure of internal negative views of the underlying assets, and like Goldman Sachs and others, continued to push out these flawed products in 2007 when it was apparent to internal officers that the market was in trouble.[75]

After the crisis, Deutsche Bank faced several lawsuits for alleged securities fraud. The bank paid U.S. regulators $145 million in November 2011 to settle allegations it misled five collapsed U.S. credit unions about risks in mortgage-backed securities. In 2011, the U.S. government accused Deutsche Bank's MortgageIT subsidiary of lying to the U.S. Department of Housing and Urban Development (HUD). The bank allegedly said its mortgage loans were eligible for federal mortgage insurance—

knowing they were not—and submitting false certification to obtain $1 billion in government insurance. Around one-third of the loans defaulted. In May 2012, Deutsche Bank paid $202.3 million to settle the civil fraud suit.[76]

In 2012, Josef Ackermann, CEO of Deutsche Bank since 2002, stepped down, after among other things, admitting the truth too slowly in the opinion of many of Deutsche Bank's investors. Ackermann had trumpeted pre-tax record profits of €10 billion and stuck to that story until October 2011 when he admitted it wasn't possible, and the stock price took a hit.[77]

Former employees became whistleblowers, and the SEC investigated allegations that Deutsche Bank did not write down $12 billion of credit derivatives losses from 2007-2010 as the market fluctuated. Bill Broeksmit had left Deutsche Bank within months after Edson died and returned in 2008 as head of portfolio risk optimization. In a 2011 presentation, Broeksmit said the allegations had no merit.

When reporter Matthew Goldstein asked me about it, I explained, "The thing about correlation desks is that it will appear you're making a lot of money from trades, but it is all money at risk. I call this kind of trading an invisible hedge fund."[78] It was easy to manipulate prices when derivatives were involved.[79]

Was Bill correct when he said the allegations had no merit? According to one of the whistleblowers, from 2008-2009, $120 billion of leveraged deals were marked as if they were unleveraged. It seemed to me that if this were true, the SEC's investigation would establish the facts of the matter.

In 2012, Anshu Jain, recruited from Merrill Lynch's derivatives area by Edson Mitchell in the 1990s, and Jürgen Hinrich Fitschen, a Citibank employee from 1975-1987, succeeded Ackerman as co-heads of Deutsche Bank. They put Broeksmit forward for the position of chief risk officer and member of the management board,[80] but Deutsche Bank's regulator, the Bundesanstalt für Finanzdienstleistungsaufsicht (BaFin), put a kibosh on Broeksmit's promotion, reportedly having doubts about him as a leader.[81]

Bill retired in February 2013 and remained an advisor until the end of that year, while Deutsche Bank faced multiple investigations into alleged evasion of sales taxes on carbon emission certificates, participation in manipulation of the London interbank offered rate (LIBOR), cosmetically using basket options to help hedge funds avoid taxes, suspect valuation of credit derivatives, poor risk controls, and more. Bill's former work was part of the evidence under examination for some of these issues.[82,83]

After he left Deutsche Bank, Josef Ackermann became chairman of Zurich Insurance. In August 2013, Zurich Insurance's CFO Pierre Wauthier, 53,

Janet Tavakoli

hung himself. Wauthier's suicide notes said he was under undue pressure at work.

Ackermann said the allegations were "unfounded" as he stepped down to safeguard the insurer's reputation. Homburger, a law firm, conducted a third-party investigation and found no evidence of undue pressure, and concluded, "We will never know the reasons for his irreversible decision."[84]

When I read the press reports of the law firm's statement, I thought Homburger might as well have just shrugged and said, *Who knows?* One can never know for certain what is in the mind of another human being, but an investigation is meant to produce a plausible theory.

Fabienne Wauthier, Pierre Wauthier's widow, confronted management at the shareholders' meeting and said her family did not accept the findings: "It was not normal pressure at the office that led to his suicide." His suicide notes said he was demoralized by the new management tone.

The new Zurich chairman, Tom de Swaan, defended the investigation and said it had been done "carefully and conclusively." Mrs. Wauthier retorted she had never been contacted by the investigator.[85] If this is true, it seems the investigation drew conclusions without being thorough.

Many admired Fabienne Wauthier's determination. She wasn't a whistleblower; she wasn't looking for money; she simply believed her husband's suicide was related to pressure at work and "we will never know" wasn't good enough for her.

60

One colleague remarked, "I wish I had someone to stick up for me like that."

The competition to produce American-style numbers that will appear pleasing to investors, the ambiguities inherent in pricing complex structured financial products, the enormous sums involved, and strong personalities who disagree about how to present those numbers create an extremely high-pressure environment that can drive a man to a nervous breakdown. Everyone in a meaningful position feels enormous stress. What may be considered undue stress by most of society is considered normal in global finance.

I met Mr. Ackermann in December 2013 when we both spoke at a business conference in Tel Aviv. He seemed a highly intelligent, pleasant, and polite man. Given Zurich Insurance's commitment to creative financial engineering and American-style results, whether Mr. Ackermann or another chairman had been in charge, it is likely that the tragic outcome for Mr. Wauthier would have been exactly the same.

Chapter 5

"Systemic Breakdown"

On January 26, 2014, Bill Broeksmit, 58, hung himself by the neck in his home in London's Evelyn Gardens. His wife discovered him when she returned home after he failed to show up for a planned restaurant lunch. She found a packet of suicide notes nearby.

Two days later, I learned of his death through *Bloomberg News*. I told the reporter that I was deeply saddened. Bill was a pioneer in interest rate swaps, and he was brilliant.[86]

There is no reason to believe Bill's death was anything other than suicide, but I was shocked by the method. Even though we hadn't been in touch for years, I recalled Bill's long-ago doubt about Roberto Calvi's so-called suicide, and in particular, his expressed aversion to death by hanging. I wondered what changed for him. Less than two years had passed since Deutsche Bank's co-heads tried—and failed to get approval—to appoint Bill chief risk officer and member of the management board. He retired in February 2013, yet remained an advisor to Deutsche Bank until just a month before his suicide. Bill didn't just kill himself, he killed himself in a way he had said he never would, and in a way he had joked about as suitable for fraudsters: a "Calvi collar."

The summer before Bill's suicide, in late June 2013, regulators from the German Central Bank known as the Bundesbank questioned ex-Deutsche Bank employees in the U.S. about the allegations that the bank incorrectly valued its massive position in credit derivatives. Press reports mentioned Bill's 2011 presentation again, including his statement that Deutsche Bank unwound most of the position and did not take heavy losses.[87]

The inquest revealed Bill met with a psychologist in July 2013, shortly after the Bundesbank's probe and a month before Zurich Insurance's Pierre Wauthier hung himself. He complained of anxiety and sleeplessness over internal investigations at Deutsche Bank. Bill was prescribed Xanax, a drug used to treat anxiety. The psychologist wrote he was "catastrophizing."[88]

Bill Broeksmit's anxiety about catastrophic scenarios had a basis in reality. The European banking system had not been recapitalized, and Deutsche Bank had internal problems and was highly leveraged.

Finance professionals under less trying circumstances than Bill's often show signs of extreme anxiety. Early in my career, I met one of the senior bond traders at a first-tier investment bank who later became a partner. He was throwing up in a trash basket, trying to keep his vomit away from his custom-tailored Italian suit. His colleagues were used to it, a mere poker tell that other traders at competing firms couldn't see.

In *Staying Sane*, Dr. Raj Persaud, who is both a psychologist and psychiatrist, talks about his patients with high anxiety:

> I have patients who are high-powered city brokers who develop panic symptoms while on the trading floor and are keen to get these resolved, as large sums of money are at stake.[89]

For Bill Broeksmit, enormous sums of money were at stake. Regulatory, government, and legal investigations were underway. As a retiree, Bill was on the outside of Deutsche Bank looking in, yet he was still deeply involved in the bank's problems, whether or not he wanted to be. Only now he had no control over his past internal work communications; he had almost no access to information about the investigations; and he had fewer, if any, colleagues to whom he could turn for information and validation.

It is hard to feel resilient if you believe you have no influence or resources to respond to investigations that may pull you into Congressional hearings, depositions, or even courtrooms. Bill knew of, and had been deeply involved in, trades that bank regulators were investigating. He knew that if regulators decide there are violations at a bank, an involved former employee sometimes becomes a scapegoat.

Bill Broeksmit was very well versed in catastrophe, as was every other long-standing finance professional. He had seen Continental Bank go under; he had seen men prosecuted and jailed after investigations into the U.S. Savings & Loan crisis. He had witnessed the roiled markets in the crash of 1987, the Russian and Mexican crises in the 1990s, the internet bubble, the panic selling in August 2007, and the financial crisis of 2008.

During the crisis, Merrill Lynch, our former mutual employer, was on the brink of collapse, and Merrill had a significant but smaller role than Goldman Sachs in AIG's collapse. Then-Treasury Secretary Hank Paulson tried to keep secret a $6.3 billion bailout payment from AIG to Merrill Lynch as he arranged a merger with Bank of America.[90]

The probability of major distress at Deutsche Bank was greater than zero, and the bank needed to raise billions of dollars. In June 2014, Deutsche Bank raised $11.6 billion in capital after offering shareholders a 24% discount to buy new stock and selling news shares on the market.[91]

On July 22, 2014, around six months after Bill Broeksmit's death, a U.S. Senate Subcommittee cited Deutsche Bank and Barclays Bank in a report about abuse of structured financial products. Broeksmit's August 25, 2009, internal email about synthetic nonrecourse prime broker facilities, written less than one year after the September 2008 financial crisis, was Exhibit 26.

He wrote how Deutsche Bank would record the legs of the trade, the economic benefits to the bank, the use of the bank's balance sheet, the risks to the bank, the tax avoidance scheme for a hedge fund—Renaissance's Medallion Fund—and that the biggest risk to Deutsche Bank would be "an August 2007 event" when hedge funds immediately deleveraged.[92] Renaissance alone used around $15 billion of Deutsche Bank's balance sheet, and Deutsche Bank earned a return on assets of around $120 million.

Hedge funds paid premiums to Deutsche Bank and Barclays Bank for so-called equity basket options with expirations longer than a year. The funds claimed long-term gains on tens of millions of short-term trades lasting only seconds. The Subcommittee estimated that from 2000 to 2013, hedge funds may have avoided $6 billion in taxes. The Subcommittee found the banks and hedge funds flouted federal leverage limits designed to limit systemic risk, the kind of risk that led to the 1928 market crash and the 2008 global banking crisis.

As I read the report, I could well imagine why Bill Broeksmit was anxious. He was deeply involved, and the tax benefits were not a slam dunk. Opinions from accountants, tax pundits, and lawyers are just that: opinions. The Senate Subcommittee recommended that the IRS audit the hedge funds and collect unpaid taxes, after disal-lowing the characterization of profits obtained from trades less than 12 months in duration as long-term gains. The Senate Subcommittee also recommended legal actions to penalize banks that engaged in tax-motivated transactions.[93]

In July 2014, news reports revealed the contents of a December 11 private letter written by Daniel Muccia, a senior vice-president of the Federal Reserve Bank of New York (FRBNY) citing a list of "material" shortcomings at Deutsche Bank that amounted to a "systemic breakdown" in a number of areas including regulatory reporting.[94]

The letter also mentioned poor technology infrastructure and "inadequate and ineffective" oversight by compliance and internal audit.

Muccia wrote: "The size and breadth of errors strongly suggest that the firm's entire US regulatory reporting structure requires wide-ranging remedial action."[95]

Deutsche Bank, Europe's third largest bank measured by tangible assets, remains highly leveraged with a weak balance sheet.[96]

Chapter 6

Influence and Decisions

September 2015 will mark the seventh anniversary of the financial crisis, yet no high-profile banker has been indicted, and the largest banks in the world still suffer from significant and avoidable management lapses.

We nurtured an ideal environment for the Fraud Triangle: need, opportunity, and the ability to rationalize one's behavior. There is dire need on Wall Street for the latest sports car, the latest tax avoidance scheme, rides on private jets, large gated homes in the Hamptons, a mistress or two on the side, a castle in Ireland, or a chateau in the south of France; the needs are unlimited. The opaque financial environment of the bloated surviving too-big-to-fail banks provides endless opportunity. Bankers don't even need to supply rationalizations, which we know from the *Big Chill* are more important than sex. Crony regulators enable fraud by providing the rationalizations for them.

Washington does not even try to come up with a decent story. In 2013, Timothy Geithner, former President of the Federal Reserve Bank of New York (2003-2009) and former United States Secretary of the Treasury (2009-2013), traveled around the country promoting his book *Stress Test*.[97],[98] In Geithner's mythology, sophisticated financiers, the so-called best and brightest, educated at our finest universities, didn't understand the dynamics of a financial bubble, and no one knew housing prices could fall. Geithner repeated this fairy tale over and over on television appearances and book tours.[99]

On May 28, 2014, Timothy Geithner and Henry Paulson gave a talk to the Chicago Council on Global Affairs about the financial crisis. Former Treasury Secretary and former Goldman Sachs CEO Hank Paulson did not mention the 100 cents on the dollar bailout of AIG that benefited Goldman Sachs at taxpayers' expense, and he did not mention how Goldman Sachs had an inside track in the negotiations. Instead, they promoted the mythology that no one saw it coming, and the only way to proceed with the bailouts was the way that Paulson and his cronies wanted it to happen. As for banking activities prior to and subsequent to the crisis, the word *fraud* never passed their lips.[100]

The ability to parse words and lie to the public has replaced financial acumen as an essential skill set in the financial industry. Malfeasance was as obvious as a woman doing a striptease in front of you on a trading floor, but

Geithner and Paulson said nothing of it, even though they very much enjoyed the show.

Geithner is now the president and managing director of Warburg Pincus, a private equity firm. Hank Paulson now lives in the building next to me in Chicago and is an esteemed member of our intellectual community, lionized as a hero of the financial crisis by mythology fans, but not so much by fans of the *Hunger Games* given that more than 46 million Americans use food stamps.[101]

I had expected Chicagoans to laugh Geithner and Paulson off the podium. Chicago is the home of investors who are still smarting from the bankruptcy of MF Global, a clearinghouse that went bankrupt under CEO Jon Corzine. Corzine had been the CEO of Goldman Sachs before Hank Paulson, and later became a State Senator and Governor of New Jersey. Investigations revealed that $1.6 billion of customer money was missing. Some of the money was impermissibly used as collateral for trades Corzine initiated for MF Global. It took years to recover the money; meanwhile, many customers were in distress. Even though there was a mountain of damaging evidence, Corzine, a top campaign bundler for the Democratic Party and a close financial confidant of Vice President Biden and President Obama, was never criminally indicted, albeit the CFTC brought a civil suit against Corzine and others.[102,103,104,105]

There seemed to be a pattern. The criminally unindicted Jon Corzine was CEO of Goldman Sachs before Hank Paulson. Hank Paulson was CEO of Goldman Sachs when the AIG trades were initiated. Robert Rubin, former co-chairman of Goldman Sachs, was a board member and strategic advisor to Citigroup before it took the largest bailout in the history of the United States. These men were financial wrecking balls.

Rather than invite executives from Goldman Sachs and other large banks to advise the White House and Congress, it would be wiser to say, *Thank you, but we think you have done enough already.*

Why have we allowed crime without punishment? When I asked Democrats close to the top of the Obama administration, their answers were so similar I thought they had memorized a script: *The administration made a bargain, and I'm not sure it was the right decision. The world was teetering on the edge of collapse. There was a crisis of confidence. There would have been unimaginable consequences.*

I believe you would have gotten a similar answer whether you asked a Republican or a Democrat; it was a bipartisan betrayal of taxpayers. Congress depends on bankers' campaign contributions, benefits from lobbyists, and a stream of lucrative jobs for friends, families, and even themselves when they leave office. Our representatives made a decision that served their own interests.

Did our representatives in Washington make the right decision for the country? They did not. They were wrong. They were dangerously and recklessly wrong. The administration tried to hide the personal benefits of this egregiously wrong decision behind a mythical idea of a "crisis of confidence" if we prosecuted, arrested, and imprisoned crooks.

There is a crisis of confidence today, but that crisis of confidence is because we did not prosecute and imprison people who defrauded the global financial markets and taxpayers.

If we indicted fraudsters, raised interest rates, and broke up too-big-to-fail banks, people would have more confidence in our government and in the financial system. Instead of sending subsidies to bankers while starving the nation of capital spending—thus diverting funds from the best way to create meaningful jobs—we could have invested in the real economy.

Raising rates would have restored confidence. If investors were paid an interest rate on Treasury bond investments that beat the inflation rate, they would have a reliable income stream and be more likely to spend that money to stimulate the economy.

Banks send a steady stream of cash back to Washington so that our elected so-called repre-sentatives make sure taxpayer money will always flow to Wall Street with no strings attached.

Taxpayers have been thoroughly and completely had.

On March 21, 2010, the Supreme Court of the United States decided *Citizens United v. Federal Election Commission.* In laymen's terms, it was deemed a violation of the First Amendment to restrict the campaign spending of corporations and unions. That paved the way for what the *New York Times* called an "exponential leap in political spending."[106]

Campaign spending was already out of control, but this decision makes it even easier. Super PACs (political action committees) are now allowed to expressly recommend voting against candidates up to Election Day—instead of the old way of just smearing candidates and halting the smears 60 days prior—though super PACs have to disclose the names of the donors, whereas the so-called social welfare groups that came before did not.

According to the Center for Responsive Politics, outside groups spent $338 million on federal elections in 2008, and in 2012, spending zoomed to over $1 billion.

Both parties have allowed contributors and lobbyists to influence them for decades. The Supreme Court decision simply made the process more efficient and expensive. Greater efficiency in a process often drives costs down—not up—but the Supreme Court is a uniquely talented, politically influenced, formerly independent branch of our government. Besides, people were complaining that Congress could be bought too cheaply.

If U.S. citizens decide to change the campaign spending status quo, it will take an amendment to the Constitution, and in addition to that, it will take an overhaul of the campaign contribution system. That process will take a very long time. It will only succeed if there is a consistent will to change a campaign system that benefits the members of Congress who would have to participate in changing it.

One of my Latin American friends compared our new crony capitalism to a banana republic: "We've seen this movie before, but this time it's in English."

You've finished. Before you go...

Tweet/share that you finished this book.

Write a brief customer review on Amazon or your favorite site for book lovers.

Give *Decisions* as a gift to your favorite financier!

Don't miss out! Visit www.janettavakoli.com and sign up for updates on Janet Tavakoli's nonbusiness books.

Visit www.tavakolistructuredfinance.com for her business blog and business book updates.

About the Author

Janet Tavakoli is the founder and president of Tavakoli Structured Finance, Inc., a Chicago-based risk consulting firm. Ms. Tavakoli has more than 20 years of experience in senior investment banking positions, trading, structuring and marketing structured financial products. She is a former adjunct associate professor of derivatives at the University of Chicago Booth Graduate School of Business. She is frequently interviewed in *The Wall Street Journal, The Financial Times, The New York Times, The Economist*, and *Bloomberg News*.

Tavakoli is the author of *Credit Derivatives and Synthetic Structures* (John Wiley & Sons, 1998, 2001), *Structured Finance & Collateralized Debt Obligations* (Wiley 2003, 2008), *Dear Mr. Buffett: What an Investor Learns 1,269 Miles from Wall Street* (Wiley 2009), *The New Robber Barons* (anthology of web articles, Lyons McNamara 2012), and *Unveiled Threat: A Personal Experience of Fundamentalist Islam and the Roots of Terrorism* (Lyons McNamara 2014). She is also the author of a financial fiction thriller, *Archangels: Rise of the Jesuits* (Lyons McNamara, 2012).

Endnotes

[1] Nick Mathiason, "Who killed Calvi?" *The Observer*, December 6, 2003.

[2] Landon Thomas, Jr., "Ex-Goldman Trader Stung in Arms Plot, Shocks Colleagues." *The Observer*, July 2, 2001. Web.

[3] Jon Burnstein, "Ex-wall Street Whiz Jailed in Cash Sting," *Sun Sentinel*, December 1, 2001. Web.

[4] Janet Tavakoli, *Credit Derivatives: A Guide to Instruments and Applications* (New York: John Wiley & Sons, 1998).

[5] Helen Dunne, "Plane crash City banker leaves wife and mistress," *The Telegraph*, December 28, 2000. Web.

[6] Associated Press, "NTSB says pilot error caused Rangeley crash; 2 died when plane hit Beaver Mountain on Dec. 22," *Bangor Daily News*, October 31, 2001.

[7] "Paid Notice: Deaths MITCHELL, EDSON V., *The New York Times*, December 16, 2000.

[8] Nils Ole Oermann, "Das Erbe nach dem Crash," *Zeit Online*. February 22, 2013.

[9] Landon Thomas, Jr., (See Note 2.)

[10] Daniel Yergin, *The Prize (*New York: Simon & Schuster, 1991).

[11] Allan Johnson, and John Gorman, "Ex-bank Executives Get Prison Terms," *Chicago Tribune*, August 31, 1988.

[12] Joshua Holland, "Hundreds of Wall Street Execs Went to Prison During the Last Fraud-Fueled Bank Crisis." Moyers & Company, September 17 2013.

[13] Michael Kirk (Producer), "The Warning," *Frontline*, PBS, October 2009.

[14] Data sources: Center for Public Integrity and Tavakoli Structured Finance, Inc.

[15] Senator Edward E. ("Ted") Kaufman, "TARP Oversight: Evaluating Returns on Taxpayer Investments," U.S. Senate Committee on Banking, March 17, 2011, P.3.

[16] Michael Burry, Interview by the Financial Crisis Inquiry Commission, May 18, 2010, (audio available online http://fcic.law.stanford.edu/resource/interviews)

[17] Michael Lewis, "Davos Is for Wimps, Ninnies, Pointless Skeptics: Michael Lewis," *Bloomberg News*, January 30, 2007.

[18] U.S. Senate Permanent Subcommittee on Investigations, "Wall Street and the Financial Crisis: Anatomy of a Financial Collapse," Washington: Government Printing Office, April 13, 2011.

[19] Mario Draghi, Address to the Harvard Kennedy School of Business, October 9, 2013.

[20] Elizabeth Warren, Jeb Hensarling, et.al., "November Oversight Report: Guarantees and Contingent Payments in TARP and Related Programs," Congressional Oversight Panel, 111th Congress, November 6, 2009.

[21] Ken Brown, and David Enrich, "Rubin, Under Fire, Defends His Role at Citi," *The Wall Street Journal*, November 29, 2008.

[22] Jody Shenn, "Bear Stearns Funds Own 67 Percent Stake in Everquest," *Bloomberg News*, May 11 2011.

[23] Matthew Goldstein, "Bear Stearns' Subprime IPO," *Business Week*, May 11, 2007.

[24] Janet Tavakoli, "The Predators' Fall." *GARP Risk Review*, March/April 07 Issue 25.

[25] Press Release 1020-136, "SEC Charges Citigroup and Two Executives for Misleading Investors About Exposure to Subprime Mortgage Assets," Securities and Exchange Commission, July 29, 2010.

[26] Ben Protess, and Peter Lattam, "A Legal Bane of Wall Street Switches Sides," *The New York Times Deal Book*, July 22, 2013.

[27] George Packer, "A Dirty Business," *The New Yorker*, June 27, 2011.

[28] Nina Bernstein, "Foes of Sex Trade Are Stung by the Fall of an Ally," *The New York Times*, March 12, 2008.

[29] Michiko Kakutani, "From 'Mr. Clean' to 'Luv Gov,'" *The New York Times Review of Books*, April 15 2010.

[30] Peter Elkind, *Rough Justice: The Rise and Fall of Eliot Spitzer* (New York: Portfolio, April 2010) P. 265.

[31] Ibid.

[32] Svea Herbst-Bayliss, "Spitzer's friend Fox upset his name used as alias," *Reuters*, March 11, 2008.

33 Lukas I. Alpert, "Eliot's Gal a Shared Asset," *New York Post*, March 16, 2008.

34 James Freeman "Crisis Management," *The Wall Street Journal*, April 5, 2011.

35 James Freeman "Eliot Spitzer and the Decline of AIG," *The Wall Street Journal*, May 16, 2008.

36 Christian Dolmetsch, "Defamation Case by Ex-AIG Boss," *Bloomberg News*, June 25, 2014.

37 Ian McDonald, Theo Francis, and Deborah Solomon, "AIG Admits 'Improper' Accounting," *The Wall Street Journal*, March 31, 2005.

38 Jill Colvin, "Eliot Spitzer Blames 'Urges' for Prostitution Scandal," *The Observer*, October 7, 2013. Web.

39 Michale Barbaro, and David W. Chen, "Spitzer Rejoins Politics, Asking for Forgiveness," *The New York Times*, July 7, 2013.

40 David M. Herszenhorn, Carl Hulse, and Sheryl Gay Stolberg, "Talks Implode During a Day of Chaos; Fate of Bailout Plan Remains Unresolved," *The New York Times*, September 25, 2008.

41 Rupert Cornwell, "Paulson was down on one knee, begging for a deal," *The Independent*, September 27, 2008.

42 SIGTARP-10-003, "Factors Affecting Efforts to Limit Payments to AIG Counterparties," Office of the Special Inspector General for the Troubled Asset Relief Program, November 17, 2009.

[43] Janet Tavakoli, "Goldman Sachs's Undisclosed Role in AIG's Distress," – Tavakoli Structured Finance, Inc., November 10, 2009.

[44] Erik Holm, and Christine Richard, "AIG's Collapse May Be Felt By Companies Worldwide," *Bloomberg News*, September 26, 2008.

[45] SIGTARP-10-003.

[46] Richard Teitelbaum, "New York Fed's Secret Choice to Pay for Swaps Hits Taxpayers," *Bloomberg News*, October 27, 2009.

[47] Gretchen Morgenson, and Don Van Natta, Jr., 'Paulson's Calls to Goldman Sachs Tested Ethics," *The New York Times*, August 8, 2009.

[48] Staff, "Lloyd Blankfein on Finding and Training the Best People," Goldman Sachs, February 2, 2012.

[49] Janet Tavakoli, "Goldman's Lies of Omission." Tavakoli Structured Finance, Inc., October 28, 2009.

[50] Janet Tavakoli, "Goldman's Undisclosed Role in AIG's Distress," Tavakoli Structured Finance, Inc., November 10, 2009.

51 Serena Ng, and Carrick Mollenkamp, "Goldman Sachs Fueled AIG Gambles, *The Wall Street Journal,* December 12, 2009. (Goldman Sachs either underwrote or bought protection in the form of credit derivatives on $33 billion of the total of $80 billion in mortgage related trades of this kind with AIG. Merrill Lynch underwrote 13.2 billion; Deutsche Bank, $9.5 billion. The previous numbers are from the WSJ's independent analysis. The article also stated: "Goldman's other big role in the CDO business that few of its competitors appreciated at the time was as an originator of CDOs that other banks invested in and that ended up being insured by AIG, a role recently highlighted by Chicago credit consultant Janet Tavakoli. Ms. Tavakoli reviewed an internal AIG document written in late 2007 listing the CDOs that AIG had insured, a document obtained earlier this year by CBS News." But the CBS News document only listed deals, not the underwriters. In addition to that document, I cross checked my data base and other data bases to determine the names of the underwriters.)

52 Richard Teitelbaum, "Secret AIG Document Shows Goldman Sachs Minted Most Toxic CDOs," *Bloomberg News*, February 23, 2010.

53 Serena Ng and Carrick Mollenkamp. (See note 51)

54 Janet Tavakoli. (See note 50.)

55 Richard Teitelbaum. (See note 52.)

56 Janet Tavakoli, "Treasury Cover-Up of Goldman's Role in AIG Crisis?" *Huffington Post*, March 18, 2010.

57 Carrick Mollenkamp, and Serena Ng, "Senate's Goldman Sachs Probe Shows Toxic Magnification," *The Wall Street Journal*, May 2, 2010. Web.

58 U.S. Senate Permanent Subcommittee on Investigations, April, 2011. (See note 18.)

59 Gretchen Morgenson, and Louise Story, "Banks Bundled Bad Debt, Bet Against It and Won," *The New York Times*, December 23, 2009.

60 Press Release 2010-123, "Goldman Sachs to Pay Record $550 Million to Settle SEC Charges Related to Subprime Mortgage CDO," Securities and Exchange Commission, July 15, 2010.

61 John Arlidge, "I'm doing 'God's work. Meet Mr Goldman Sachs," *Sunday Times*, November 8, 2009.

62 David Reilly, "In Subprime, AIG Sees Small Risk; Others See More," *The Wall Street Journal*, August 13, 2007.

63 Amir Efrati, and Liam Pleven, "SEC, Justice Scrutinize AIG on Swaps Accounting," *The Wall Street Journal*, June 6, 2008.

64 Joshua Zumbrun, "What AIG Really Owes Taxpayers," *Forbes*, September 1, 2009. Web.

65 Lynnley Browning, "How the NY Fed Bent the Rules for Citibank," *Newsweek*, December 22, 2014.

66 Zachary A. Goldfarb, and Jonathan Mummolo, "A Life Lost in the Shadow of Freddie Mac's Turmoil," *The Washington Post,* April 23, 2009.

67 Charles Duhigg, and Jack Healy, "Reported Suicide Is Latest Shock at Freddie Mac," *The New York Times*, April 22, 2009.

68 Kara Scannell, "FASB Eases Mark-to-Market Rules," *The Wall Street Journal*, April 3, 2009.

[69] Dawn Kopecki, "Blythe Masters Says 'Don't Panic' as Commodities Slip," *BloombergBusiness*, August 3, 2010. Web.

[70] Janet Tavakoli, "JPMorgan's and Blythe Masters' Debacles in Commodities," Tavakoli Structured Finance, Inc., August 9, 2010. Web.

[71] Agustino Fontevecchio, "JP Morgan Top Exec Blythe Masters Dodges Penalty As Bank Settles Energy Manipulation Charges for $410M," *Forbes*, July 30, 2013. Web.

[72] Janet Tavakoli, "A Risk Manager's Impossibility?" *Risk News and Resources* (with limited permission ©Tavakoli Structured Finance, Inc.), September 24, 2013.

[73] U.S. Senate Permanent Subcommittee on Investigations Committee on Homeland Security and Government Affairs, "JPMorgan Whale Trades: A Case History of Derivatives Risks and Abuses," Washington: Government Printing Office, March 14, 2013, P. 17.

[74] James Saft, "Why Jamie Dimon is richer than you," *Reuters*, February 27, 2013.

[75] U.S. Senate Permanent Subcommittee on Investigations. (See note 73.)

[76] Grant McCook, "Deutsche Bank to pay $202 million U.S. mortgage settlement," *Reuters,* May 10, 2012.

[77] Stefan Kaiser, "Deutsche Bank Throws in Towel," *Spiegel Online*, November 15, 2011. Web.

[78] Matthew Goldstein, "Exclusive: Deutsche Bank's firing of top trader sparks probe," *Reuters*, June 24, 2011.

[79] Janet Tavakoli, "The Elusive Income of Synthetic CDOs," *The Journal of Structured Finance*, Winter 2006 Volume 11, Number 4.

[80] Landon Thomas, Jr., "Changes at Top of Deutsche Bank Start to Come Into Focus," *The New York Times Deal Book*, March 7, 2012.

[81] Larry Arnold, and Nicholas Comfort, "William Broeksmit, Ex-Deutsche Bank Risk Manager, Dies at 58," *Bloomberg News*, January 28, 2014.

[82] Jack Ewing, "Top Deutsche Bank Executives Caught Up in Tax Evasion Inquiry," *The New York Times Dealbook*, December 12, 2012.

[83] Alexander Huebner, Kathrin Jones, and Christoph Steitz, "Bafin exonerates Deutsche Bank's Jain in Libor probe: Handelsblatt," *Reuters*, December 7, 2014.

[84] Katharina Bart, "Exclusive: Widow of Zurich CFO to confront insurer at AGM over suicide," *Reuters*, April 1, 2014.

[85] Alan Tovey, "Zurich Insurance executive's widow confronts company's annual meeting," *The Telegraph*, April 2, 2014.

[86] Ibid. Larry Arnold, "William Broeksmit" (see note 81.)

[87] Staff, "Bundesbank questions ex-Deutsche Bank employees in U.S. – sources." *Reuters*, June 27, 2013.

[88] Ben Moshinsky, "Broeksmit Was 'Anxious' About Probes Before Suicide," *Bloomberg News*, March 25, 2014.

[89] Raj Persaud, *Staying Sane* (London: Metro Books, 1997) P. 277.

90 Liz Rappaport, "Lewis Testifies U.S. Urged Silence on Deal," *The Wall Street Journal*, April 23, 2009.

91 Nicholas Comfort, "Deutsche Bank Offers Stock in $11.6 Billion Capital Boost," *Bloomberg News*, June 5, 2014. Web.

92 U.S. Senate Permanent Subcommittee on Investigations Committee on Homeland Security and Government Affairs, "Abuse of Structured Financial Products," Washington: Government Printing Office, July 22, 2014.

93 Ibid.

94 David Enrich, Jenny Strasburg, and Eyk Henning, "Deutsche Bank Suffers From Litany of Reporting Problems, Regulators Say," *The Wall Street Journal*, July 22, 2014. Web.

95 Camilla Hall, and Gina Chon, "NY Fed hits at Deutsche Bank's 'unreliable' regulatory reports," *The Financial Times*, July 22, 2014. Web.

96 Staff, "A Weary Lender," *The Economist*, November 1, 2014.

97 Timothy F. Geithner, *Stress Test: Reflections on the Financial Crisis* (New York: Crown, May 2014).

98 Dylan Byers, "Geithner taps Time's Grunwald for new book," *Dylan Byers on Media*, May 24, 2013. Web. (Rumor mongers claimed Geithner paid his ghost writer $300,000.)

99 Timothy Geithner, and Jon Stewart, "Exclusive – Timothy Geithner Extended Interview," *The Daily Show*, Comedy Central, May 21, 2014, @26:38 to 30:30 of the full extended interview.

100 Timothy Geithner, and Henry Paulson, "Reflections on the Financial Crisis," Address to the Chicago Council on Global Affairs, May 28, 2014.

101 Allison Linn, "Who Uses Food Stamps? Millions of Children," NBC News, March 17, 2014.

102 Kevin McCoy, "Regulators sue Corzine over MF Global collapse," *USA Today*, June 28, 2013.

103 Joseph Checkler, "Judge Allows Corzine and Others to Tap MF Global Insurance," *The Wall Street Journal*, September 5, 2014.

104 *U.S. Commodity Futures Trading Commission v. MF Global Inc., MF Global Holdings LTD., Jon S. Corzine, and Edith O'Brian* (13 CIV 4463), June 27, 2013.

105 Conor Friedersdorf, "Obama's Team Relied on Jon Corzine for Economic Advice," *The Atlantic*, November 14, 2013.

106 Matt Bai, "How Much Has Citizens United Changed the Political Game?" *The New York Times*, July 17, 2012.

Made in the USA
Middletown, DE
05 January 2018